GRAPHIC OrgaNiZeRs FOR READING

IncentivePublications

Written by Kathleen Bullock, Cherrie Farnette,
Marjorie Frank, Jill Norris, and Kris Sexton
Edited by Cary Grayson

ISBN 978-0-86530-034-7

6   7   8   9   10   15   14   13   12

Printed by Sheridan Books, Inc., Chelsea, Michigan • September 2012
www.incentivepublications.com

Using Graphic Organizers

The use of graphic organizers makes it easier for students to comprehend and remember what they read. Graphic organizers help students:

- visualize abstract content,
- connect new ideas to previous knowledge,
- identify main ideas and supporting details,
- understand sequences,
- recognize relationships,
- focus on specific elements,
- compare ideas and concepts, and
- recall and retrieve information.

Scientifically-based research shows that using graphic organizers leads to improved student performance on assessments and enhanced critical thinking skills. The National Reading Panel (2000) cited graphic and semantic organizers as one of the most effective ways to help students improve reading comprehension.

Graphic Organizers for Reading is one resource every teacher needs. Here are 60 graphic organizers for fiction and nonfiction, literary elements and genre, and reading in any content area. Use the organizers to reinforce important reading strategies.

Help students organize for success!

Graphic Organizers for Reading Comprehension and Analysis
pages 3–40

Graphic Organizers for Studying Genre
pages 41–52

Graphic Organizers for Yourself
pages 53–64

Graphic Organizers

for
Reading Comprehension and Analysis

Character Wheel 4

Short Story Guide 5

Story Map 6

Storyline 7

Plot Links 8

A Staircase of Events 9

Setting 10

Word Net 11

Mood 12

Storyteller's Role 13

Author's Toolbox 14

Actions and Reactions 15

Personal Connections 16

Character Squares 17

Good vs. Evil 18

Making Predictions 19

Thinking About the Author 20

Thinking About the Illustrator 21

Identifying Cause and Effect 22

Follow the Clues 23

Understanding Symbols 24

Nonfiction Reading Guide 25

Main Idea and Details 26

Now and Then Mandala 27

Fact Finder 28

Purpose, Important Ideas, Connections 29

Reading Survey 30

KWL 31

KWHL 32

Reading the Visuals 33

Research Map 34

Chapter Map Study Guide 35

Signal Words 36

Comparing Two Stories 37

3-2-1 38

The End 39

Give Me Five (+ One) 40

CHARACTER WHEEL

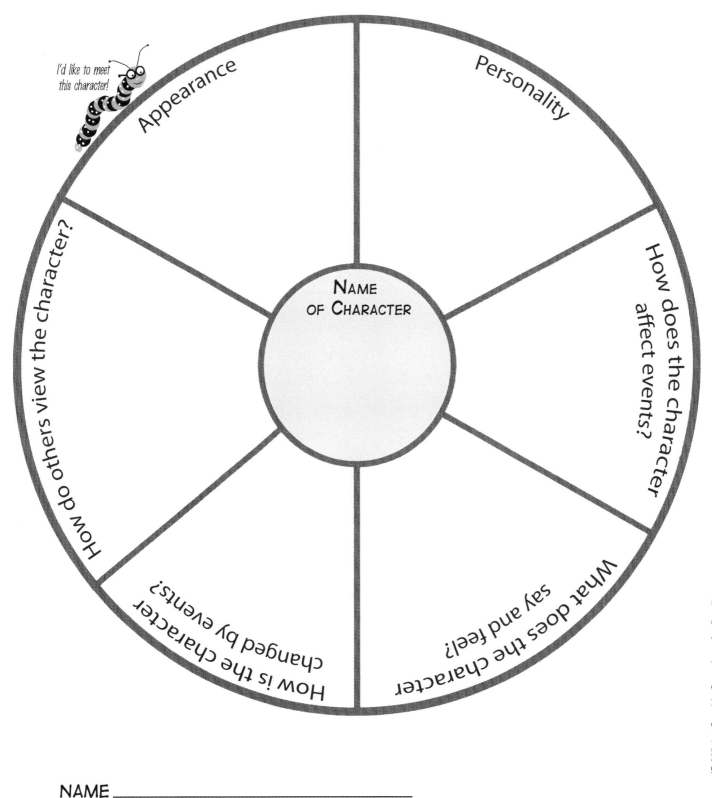

I'd like to meet this character!

Appearance

Personality

How does the character affect events?

What does the character say and feel?

How is the character changed by events?

How do others view the character?

NAME OF CHARACTER

NAME _____

IP 925-1 • *Graphic Organizers for Reading*
Copyright ©2006 by Incentive Publications, Inc., Nashville, TN.

SHORT STORY GUIDE

NAME

TITLE AND AUTHOR

HOOK

CONFLICT

AUTHOR'S TECHNIQUES

SETTING

RESOLUTION

MY PERSONAL RESPONSE

CHARACTERS

What a bunch
of characters!

IP 925-1 • *Graphic Organizers for Reading*
Copyright © 2006 by Incentive Publications, Inc., Nashville, TN.

Name _____

Story Map

Title

Author

Setting

Time

Place

Plot Summary

Words to Remember

Be-e a smart reader!

Character Name
_____
Description

Role in Story

Character Name
_____
Description

Role in Story

Character Name
_____
Description

Role in Story

Character Name
_____
Description

Role in Story

Character Name
_____
Description

Role in Story

6

IP 925-1 • Graphic Organizers for Reading
Copyright ©2006 by Incentive Publications, Inc., Nashville, TN.

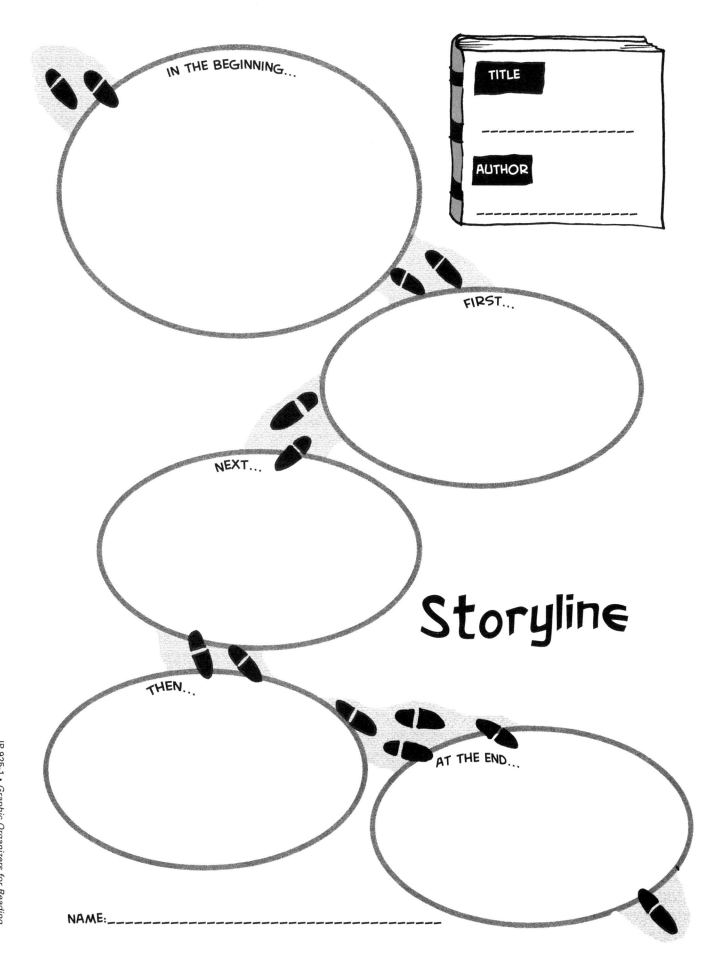

IN THE BEGINNING...

TITLE

_____

AUTHOR

_____

FIRST...

NEXT...

Storyline

THEN...

AT THE END...

IP 925-1 • Graphic Organizers for Reading
Copyright © 2006 by Incentive Publications, Inc., Nashville, TN.

NAME:_____

PLOT LINKS

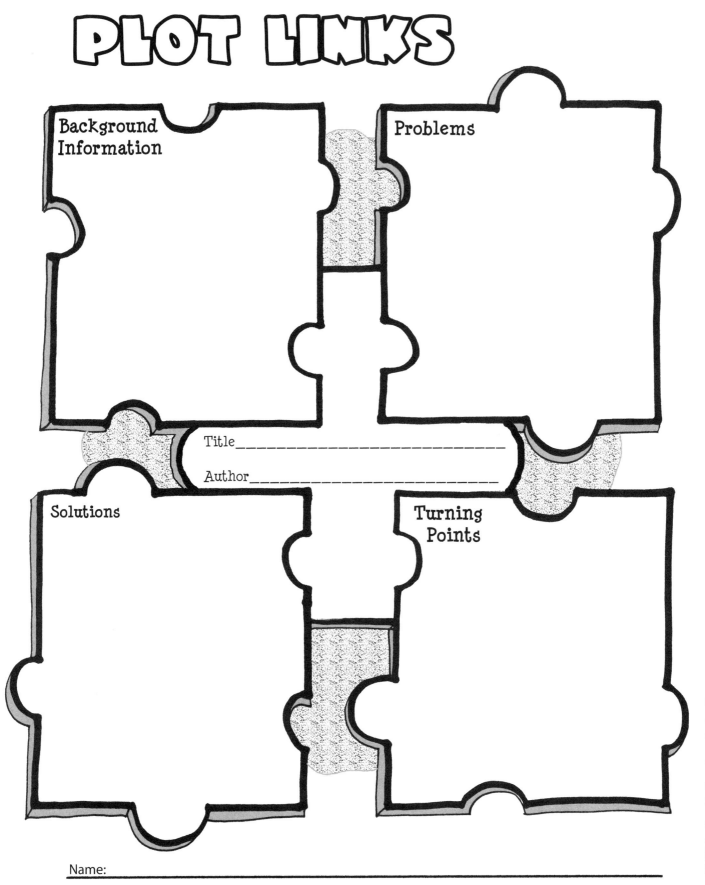

Background Information

Problems

Title_____

Author_____

Solutions

Turning Points

Name: _____

IP 925-1 • *Graphic Organizers for Reading*
Copyright ©2006 by Incentive Publications, Inc., Nashville, TN.

A STAIRCASE OF EVENTS

Title: _____

Author: _____

Sequence of Events

Starting Point

Climax

Plot Action

Resolution

Name: _____

IP 925-1 • _Graphic Organizers for Reading_
Copyright ©2006 by Incentive Publications, Inc., Nashville, TN.

TITLE:_____   AUTHOR:_____

SETTING

PLACE	TIME

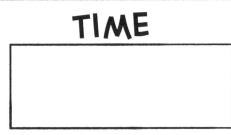

PLACE

```
┌──────────────────┐
│                  │
│                  │
│                  │
└──────────────────┘
```

•

•

•

•

TIME

```
┌──────────────────┐
│                  │
│                  │
│                  │
└──────────────────┘
```

•

•

•

•

NAME:_____

IP 925-1 • *Graphic Organizers for Reading*
Copyright ©2006 by Incentive Publications, Inc., Nashville, TN.

Name _____

Title _____

Author _____

Word Net

Catch words you want to remember.

IP 925-1 • *Graphic Organizers for Reading*
Copyright ©2006 by Incentive Publications, Inc., Nashville, TN.

TITLE: _____   AUTHOR: _____

CHARACTER'S
ATTITUDES

ATMOSPHERE OF THE
SETTING

EFFECTS OF
EVENTS ON MOOD

MOOD

WRITE A DESCRIPTION HERE.

DOES THE MOOD
CHANGE DURING THE STORY?

NAME: _____

IP 925-1 • *Graphic Organizers for Reading*

Title:_____   Author:_____

What is the storyteller's role?

Storyteller:_____

☐ **All-Knowing Observer –**
An outside voice understands all the character's emotions and tells the story.

☐ **Objective Reporter –**
A detached observer reports the facts.

☐ **First Person –**
A character tells the story from a personal point of view.

☐ **Third Person –**
An outside voice tells and comments on characters and the story.

Give examples that support your answer.

Example

Example

Example

How does the point of view affect your response to this story?_____

_____

_____

_____

Name:_____

IP 925-1 • *Graphic Organizers for Reading*
Copyright © 2006 by Incentive Publications, Inc., Nashville, TN.

AUTHOR'S TOOLBOX

METAPHORS	SIMILES	PERSONIFICATION
PICTURE LANGUAGE	ALLITERATION	EXPLICIT VERBS

MY REACTION:

TITLE_____

AUTHOR_____

NAME:_____

IP 925-1 • *Graphic Organizers for Reading*
Copyright ©2006 by Incentive Publications, Inc., Nashville, TN.

Actions and REACTIONS

Title_____   Author_____

Action

Reaction

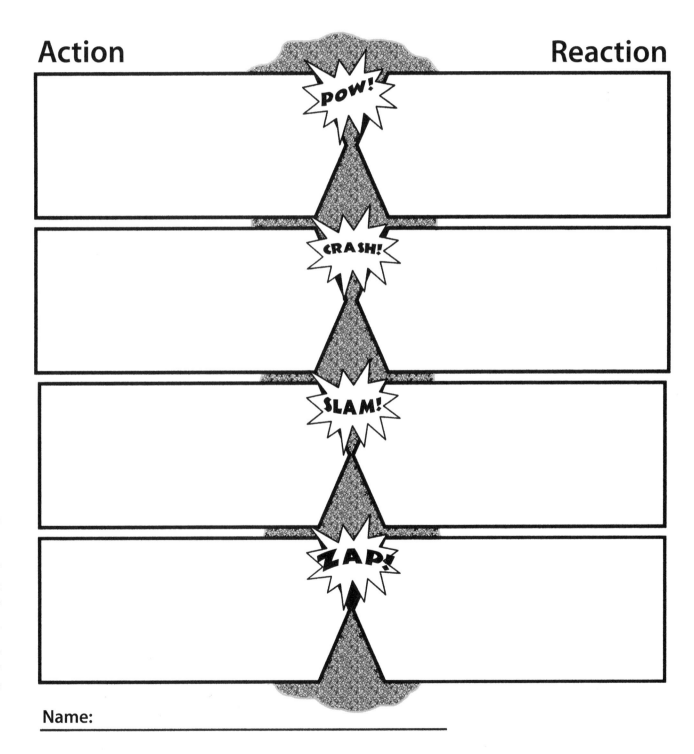

Name: _____

IP 925-1 • *Graphic Organizers for Reading*
Copyright ©2006 by Incentive Publications, Inc., Nashville, TN.

Personal Connections

It happened to_____
                        (character's name)

in_____ .
                        (title)

It happened here_____ .
                        (setting)

This is what happened:

It happened to me when I was_____ .
                        (age)

It happened to me here_____ .
                        (setting)

This is what happened:

Name:_____

IP 925-1 • *Graphic Organizers for Reading*
Copyright ©2006 by Incentive Publications, Inc., Nashville, TN.

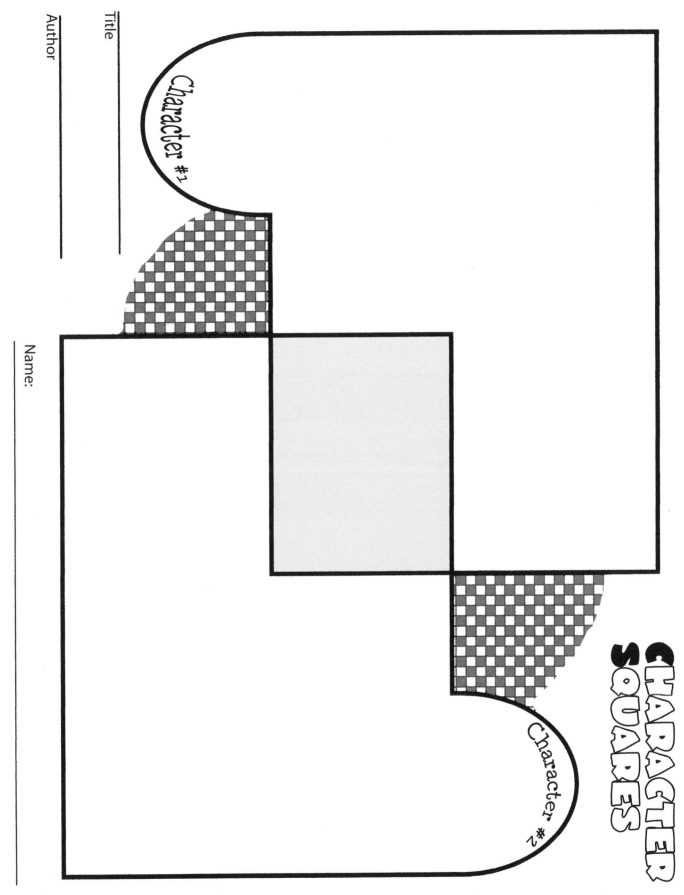

Title

Author

Name:

Character #1

Character #2

CHARACTER SQUARES

IP 925-1 • Graphic Organizers for Reading
Copyright © 2006 by Incentive Publications, Inc., Nashville, TN.

Good vs. Evil

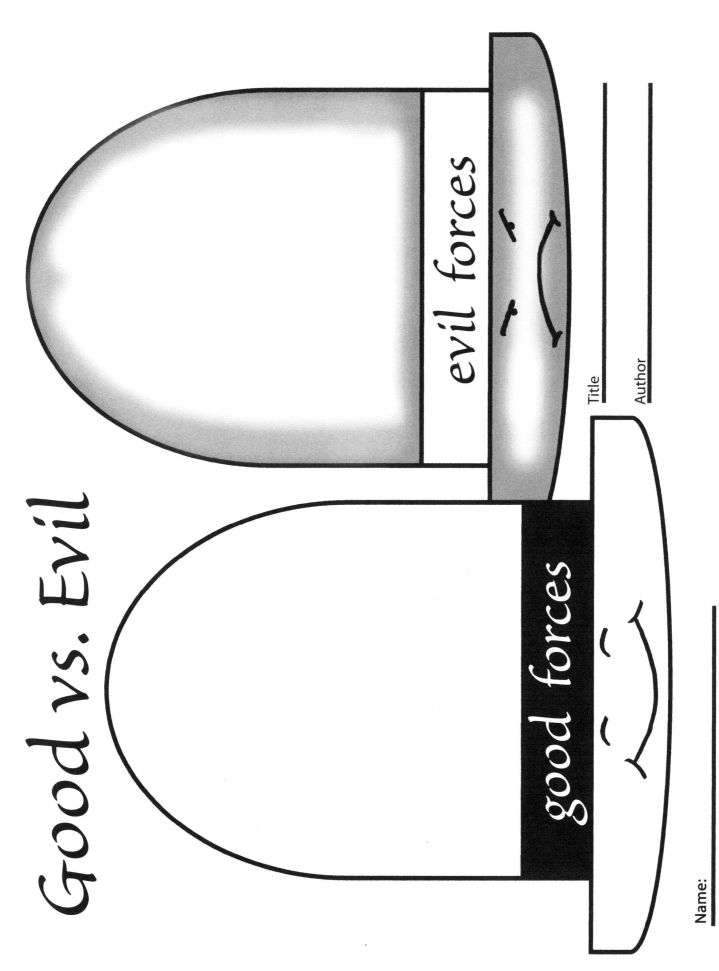

evil forces

good forces

Title

Author

Name:

IP 925-1 • *Graphic Organizers for Reading*

MAKING PREDICTIONS

I THINK THIS WILL HAPPEN...   THIS HAPPENED...

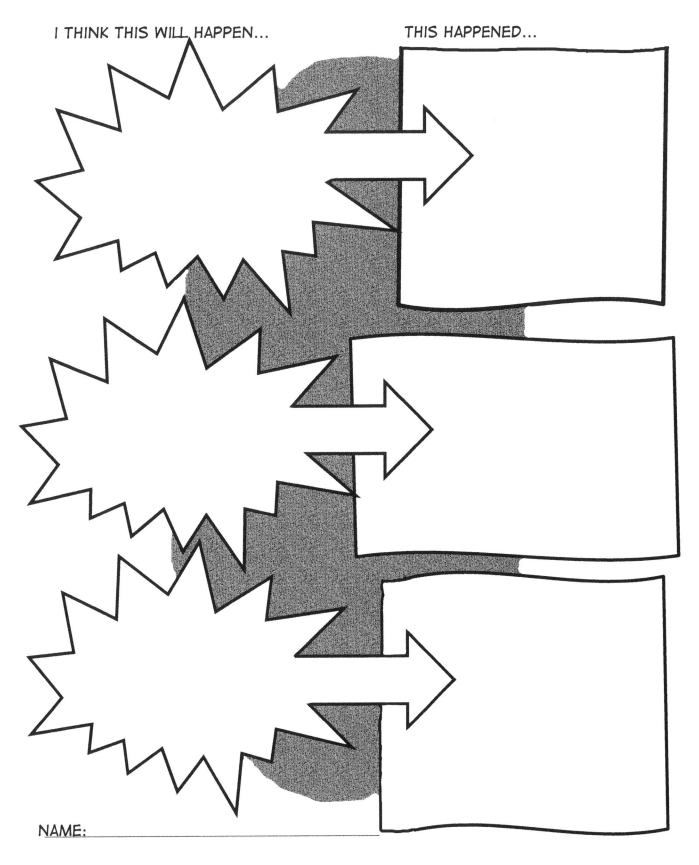

NAME: _____

Thinking About the Author

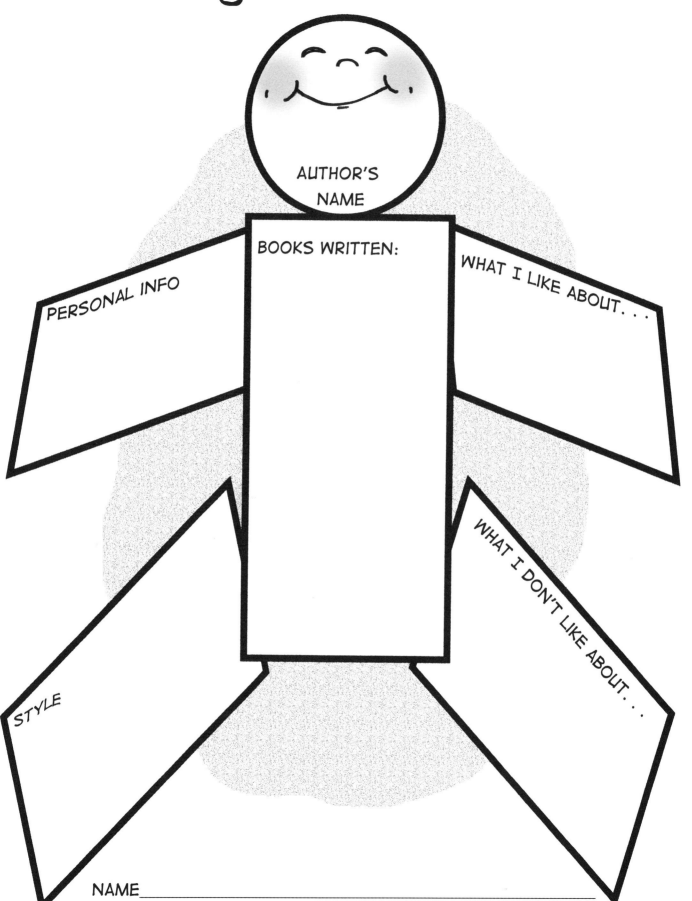

AUTHOR'S NAME

BOOKS WRITTEN:

PERSONAL INFO

WHAT I LIKE ABOUT . . .

WHAT I DON'T LIKE ABOUT . . .

STYLE

NAME_____

IP 925-1 • *Graphic Organizers for Reading*

Thinking About the Illustrator

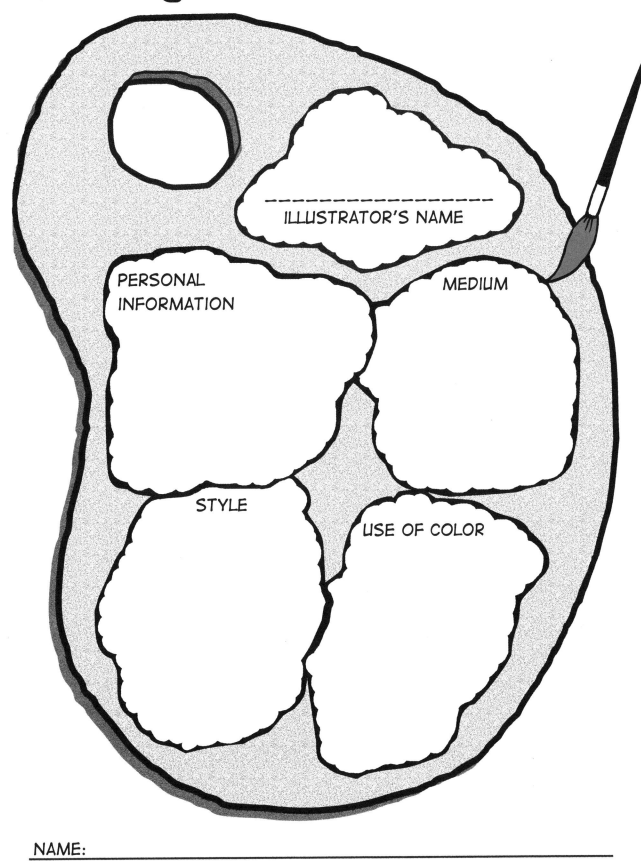

ILLUSTRATOR'S NAME

PERSONAL INFORMATION

MEDIUM

STYLE

USE OF COLOR

NAME: _____

IP 925-1 • *Graphic Organizers for Reading*
Copyright © 2006 by Incentive Publications, Inc., Nashville, TN.

IDENTIFYING CAUSE AND EFFECT

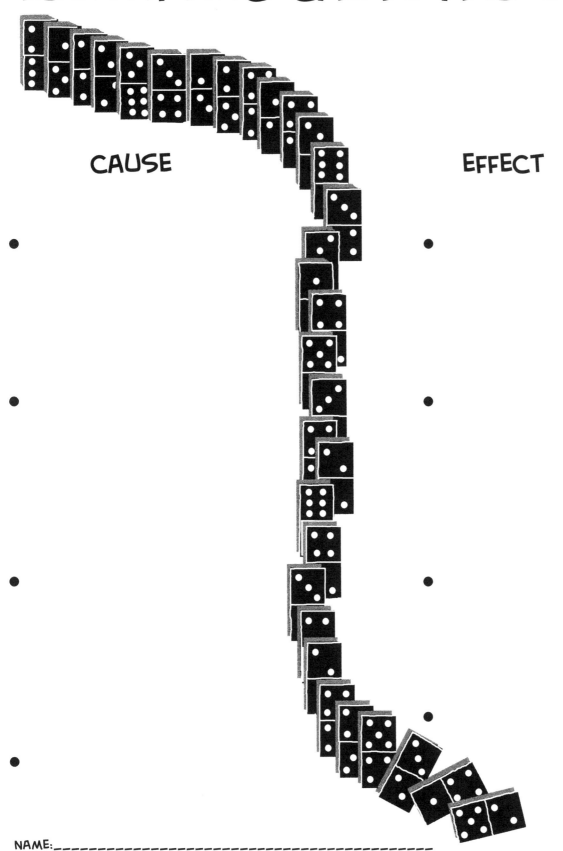

CAUSE

EFFECT

NAME:_____

IP 925-1 • *Graphic Organizers for Reading*
Copyright ©2006 by Incentive Publications, Inc., Nashville, TN.

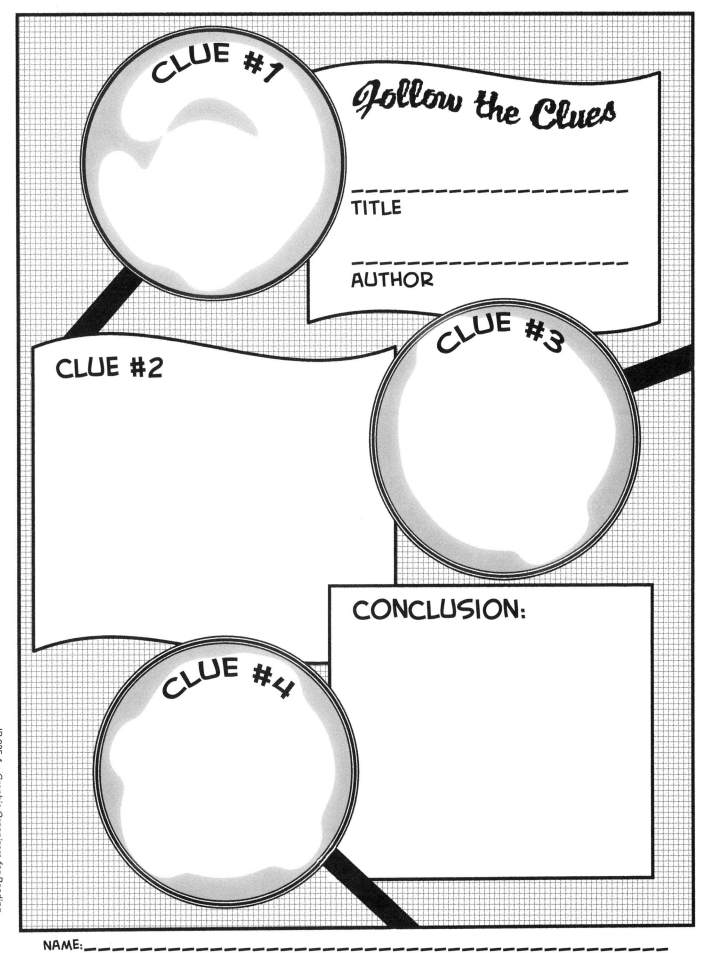

CLUE #1

Follow the Clues

_ _ _ _ _ _ _ _ _ _ _ _ _ _ _ _ _ _ _ _
TITLE

_ _ _ _ _ _ _ _ _ _ _ _ _ _ _ _ _ _ _ _
AUTHOR

CLUE #3

CLUE #2

CONCLUSION:

CLUE #4

NAME: _

Understanding symbols

THE SYMBOLS

Symbols are concrete objects that stand for an idea.

In literature, ladybugs are symbols of mother love.

WHAT THEY MEAN

Give an example from the story.

Some authors use the bee as a symbol of industriousness.

Title _____

Author _____

IP 925-1 • *Graphic Organizers for Reading*

NONFICTION READING GUIDE

NAME _____

TITLE _____

AUTHOR _____

AUDIENCE

PURPOSE

MAIN IDEA

SUPPORTING DETAILS

MAIN IDEA

SUPPORTING DETAILS

MY REACTION

I've got the reading bug!

IP 925-1 • *Graphic Organizers for Reading*
Copyright © 2006 by Incentive Publications, Inc., Nashville, TN.

MAIN IDEA

The main idea must be supported by details or the whole web will collapse.

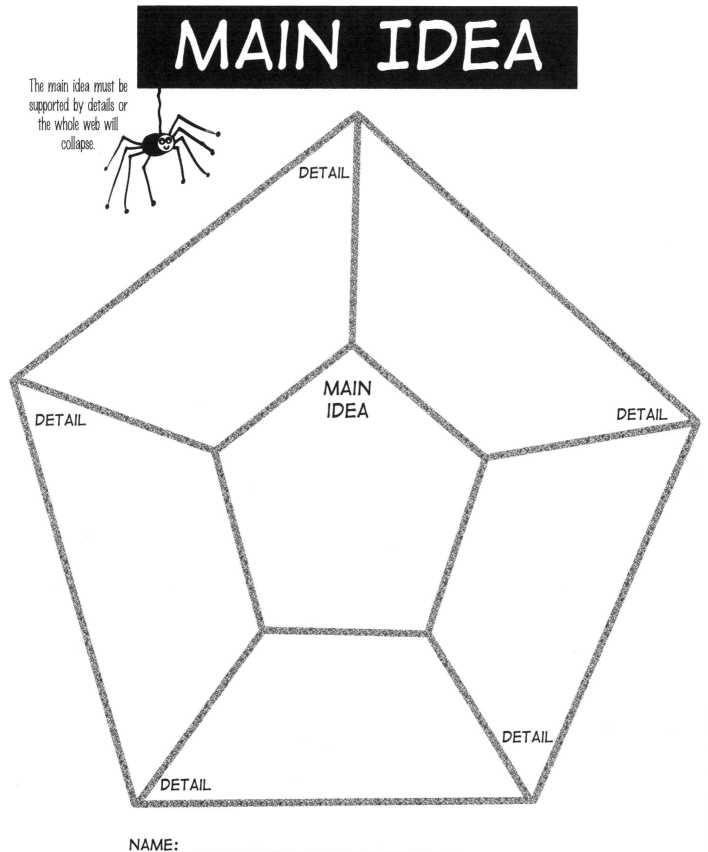

DETAIL

DETAIL

MAIN IDEA

DETAIL

DETAIL

DETAIL

DETAIL

NAME:_____

IP 925-1 • *Graphic Organizers for Reading*

Reading About History

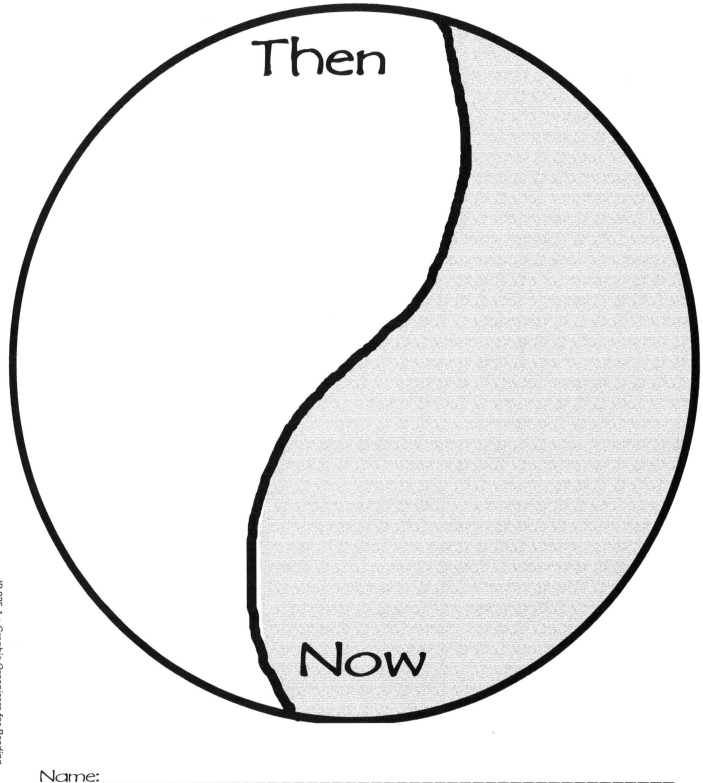

Then

Now

Name:_____

fact finder

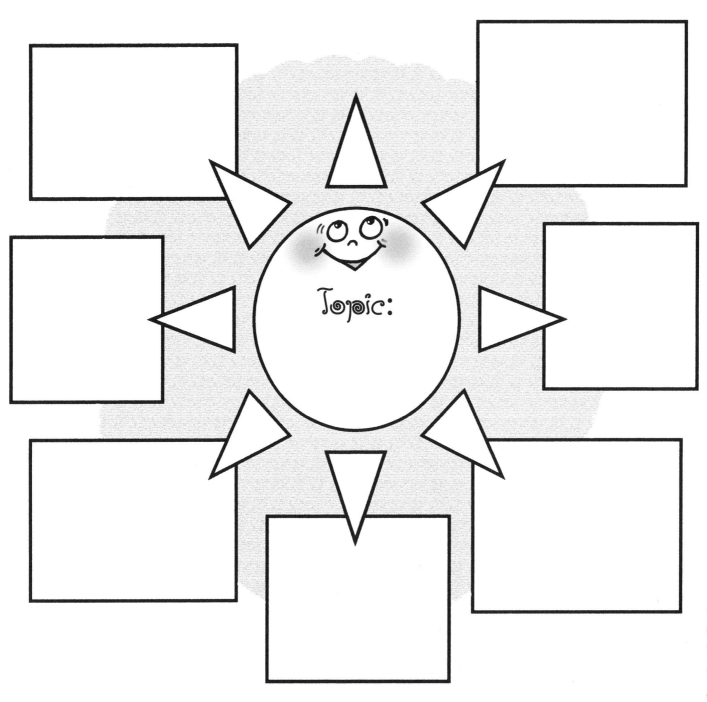

Topic:

Name: _____

IP 925-1 • *Graphic Organizers for Reading*

As I read, I'll think about...

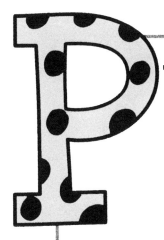

Purpose   Write your purpose for reading here.

Important Ideas   Write three or four ideas, words, or concepts you learned here.

Connections Write about the connections between what you learned and what you already knew.

Name:_____

Reading Survey

1. LOOK AT THE TITLE. ☐
2. READ THE INSTRUCTIONS. ☐
3. READ THE MAIN HEADINGS. ☐
4. READ THE FIRST AND LAST PARAGRAPHS. ☐
5. READ THE SUMMARY.
   WRITE A SUMMARY IN YOUR OWN WORDS.

_____

_____

_____

_____

_____

_____

6. IDENTIFY THE SOURCE.

_____

NAME: _____

IP 925-1 • Graphic Organizers for Reading

K W L

I am keen, wise, and literate.

WHAT I KNOW	WHAT I WANT TO KNOW	WHAT I LEARNED
K	**W**	**L**
BEFORE READING	BEFORE READING	AFTER READING

NAME:_____

K W H L

A wise owl knows how to learn.

WHAT I **K**NOW	WHAT I **W'**ANT TO KNOW	**H**OW I CAN FIND THE INFORMATION	WHAT I **L**EARNED
BEFORE READING	BEFORE READING	DURING READING	AFTER READING

NAME: _____

IP 925-1 • *Graphic Organizers for Reading*

READING THE VISUALS

ILLUSTRATIONS AND PHOTOS	MAPS	CHARTS
page_____	page_____	page_____
page_____	page_____	page_____
page_____	page_____	page_____

RESEARCH MAP

TOPIC

SOURCE

SOURCE

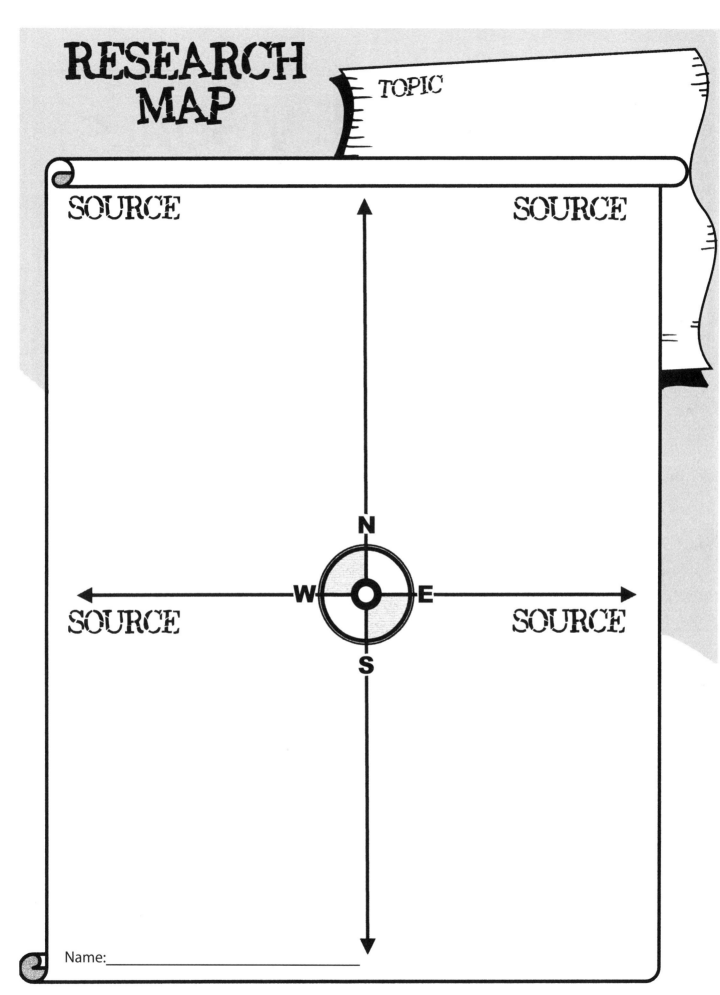

N

W   E

S

SOURCE

SOURCE

Name: _____

34

CHAPTER MAP
STUDY GUIDE

TITLE _____

CHAPTER _____

MAIN IDEA

IMPORTANT DETAILS

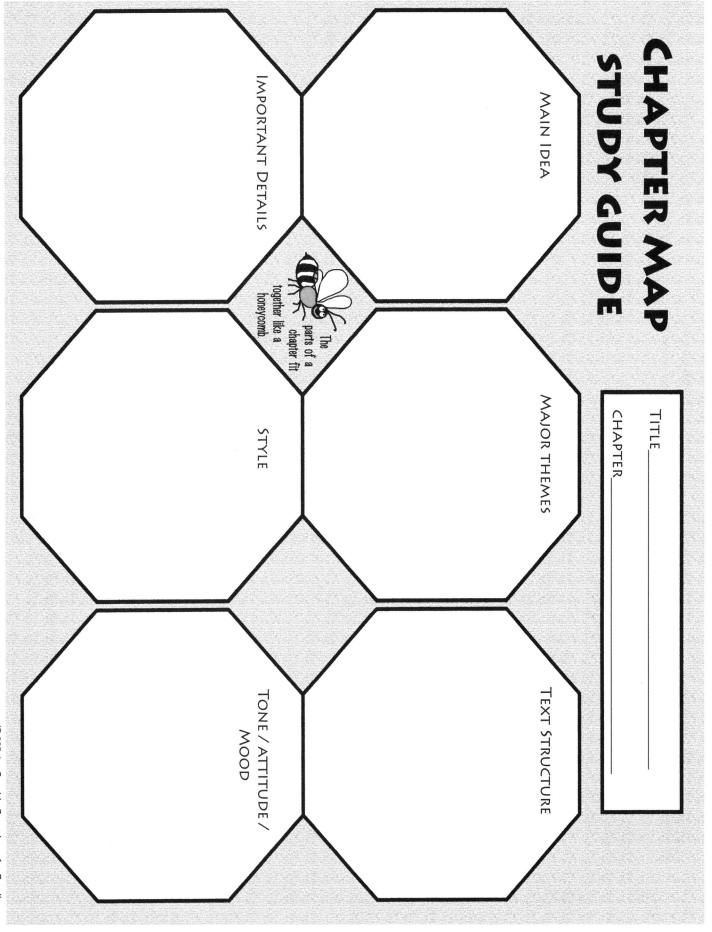

The parts of a chapter fit together like a honeycomb

MAJOR THEMES

STYLE

TEXT STRUCTURE

TONE / ATTITUDE / MOOD

NAME:_____

IP 925-1 • *Graphic Organizers for Reading*
Copyright ©2006 by Incentive Publications, Inc., Nashville, TN.

SIGNAL WORDS

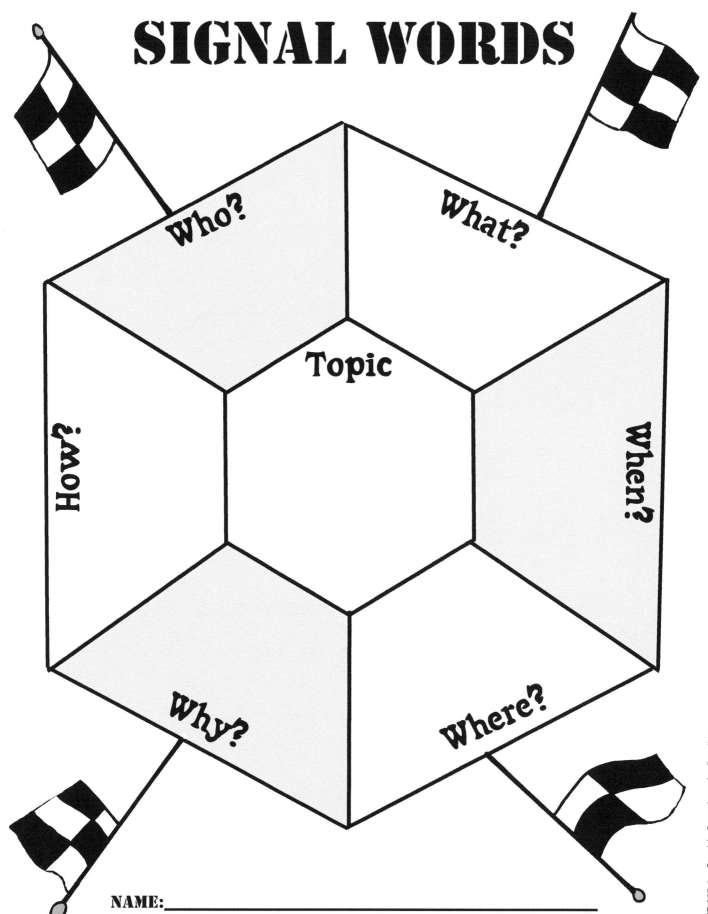

Who?

What?

How?

When?

Topic

Why?

Where?

NAME:_____

IP 925-1 • *Graphic Organizers for Reading*
Copyright ©2006 by Incentive Publications, Inc., Nashville, TN.

COMPARING TWO STORIES

STORY 1: _____   STORY 2: _____

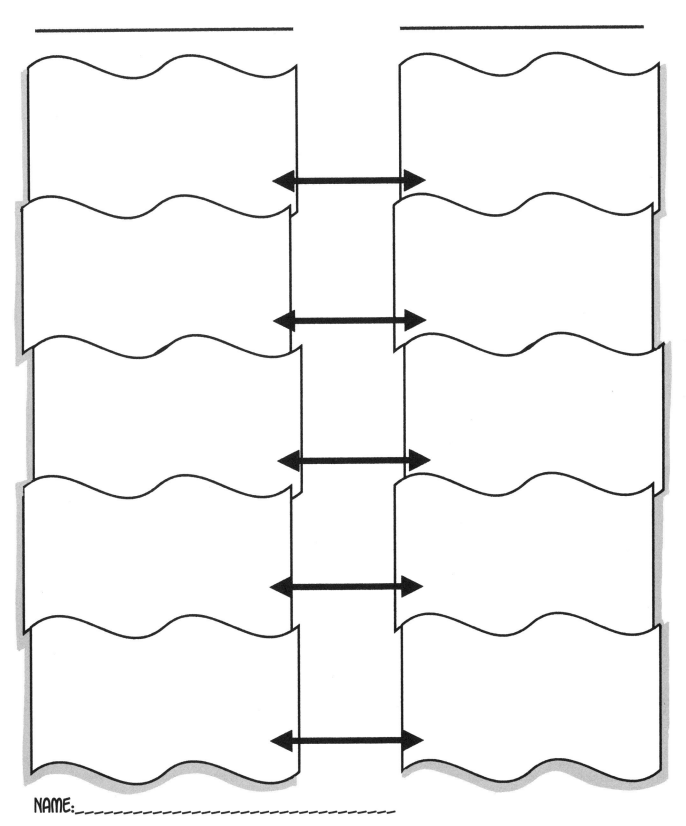

NAME:_____

NAME:_____

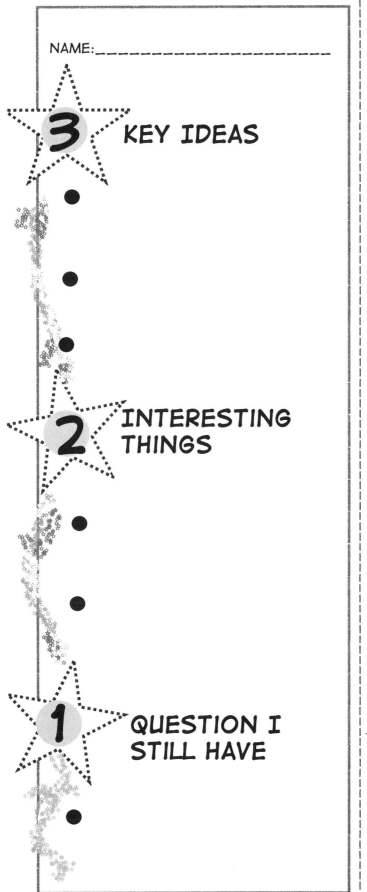

3 KEY IDEAS

•

•

•

2 INTERESTING THINGS

•

•

1 QUESTION I STILL HAVE

•

NAME:_____

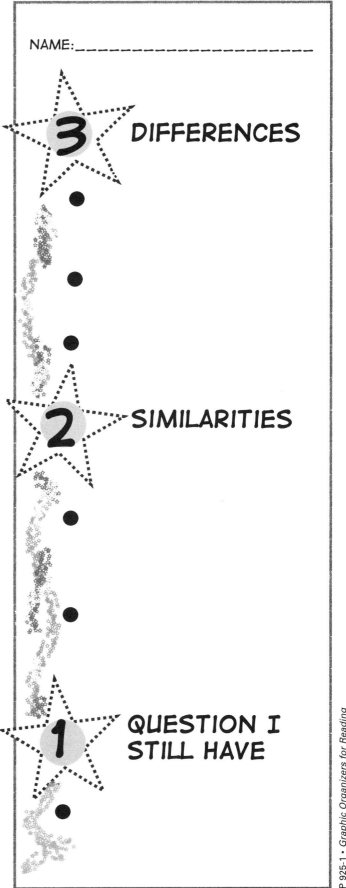

3 DIFFERENCES

•

•

•

2 SIMILARITIES

•

•

1 QUESTION I STILL HAVE

•

IP 925-1 • *Graphic Organizers for Reading*
Copyright ©2006 by Incentive Publications, Inc., Nashville, TN.

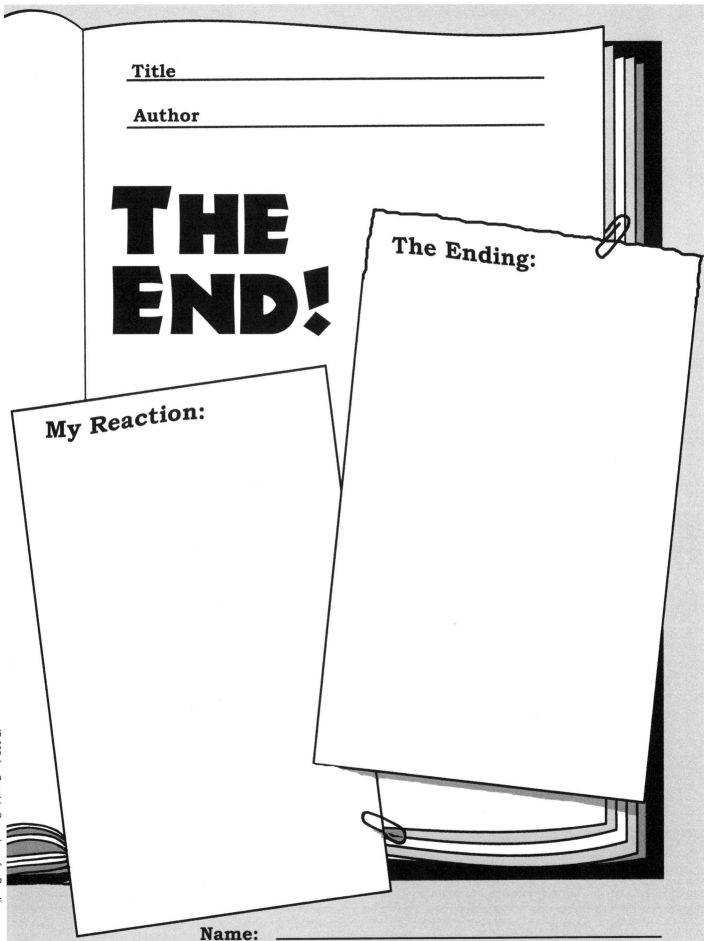

Title _____

Author _____

THE END!

The Ending:

My Reaction:

Name: _____

IP 925-1 • *Graphic Organizers for Reading*
Copyright © 2006 by Incentive Publications, Inc., Nashville, TN.

GIVE ME FIVE (+ ONE)

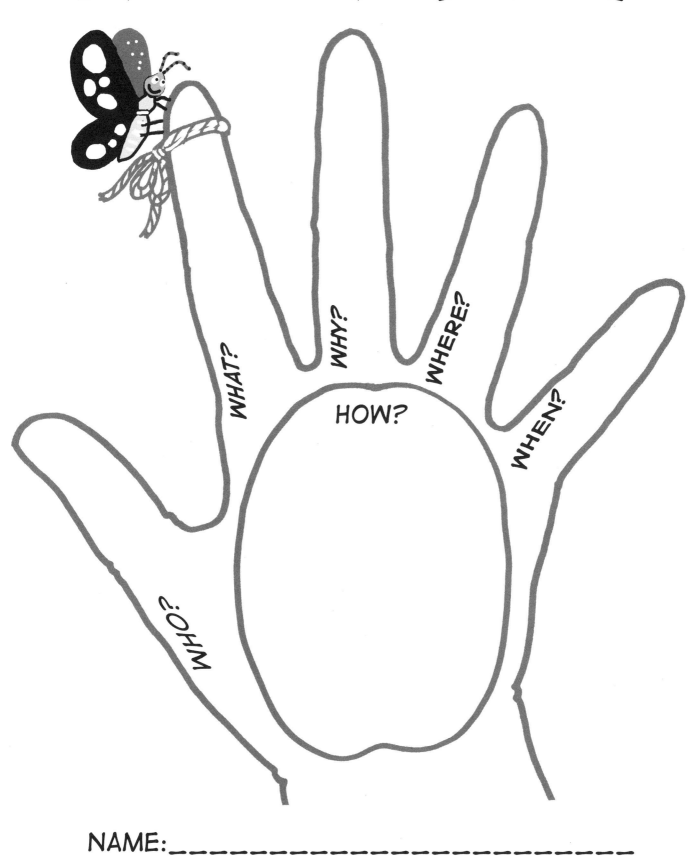

WHAT?

WHY?

WHERE?

WHEN?

HOW?

WHO?

NAME:_____

IP 925-1 • *Graphic Organizers for Reading*
Copyright ©2006 by Incentive Publications, Inc., Nashville, TN.

Graphic Organizers
for
Studying Genre

Mysteries 42

Poetry 43

Realistic Fiction 44

Science Fiction 45

Biographies 46

Animal Stories 47

Fables 48

Fairy Tales 49

Fantasy 50

Historical Fiction 51

Humor 52

Mysteries

Important Mystery in Story:

Attributes of Mysteries

- ☐ Problem or crime to solve
- ☐ Protagonist solves the mystery.
- ☐ Clues are provided.
- ☐ A wrongdoer is revealed.
- ☐ Innocent suspects

Clues to Its Solution:

Solution:

Were You Surprised? Why or Why Not?

Name _____

IP 925-1 • *Graphic Organizers for Reading*
Copyright ©2006 by Incentive Publications, Inc., Nashville, TN.

Poetry

The Subject of the Poem:

What It Says To Me:

Attributes of Poetry

- ☐ A few powerful words
- ☐ Strong images or emotions
- ☐ Made-up words or phrases
- ☐ Rhyme or rhythm
- ☐ Repetition or patterns

NEVERMORE

Examples of Elements

Rhyme	Images
Rhythm	Words

Name _____

Realistic Fiction

Setting:

Characters:

Name   Role in Story

Attributes of Realistic Fiction

- ☐ Story events could really happen.
- ☐ The characters seem real.
- ☐ The setting seems real.
- ☐ The details seem real.
- ☐ I learn about myself and others as I read.

Story Events

Real Events

Name _____

IP 925-1 • *Graphic Organizers for Reading*
Copyright © 2006 by Incentive Publications, Inc., Nashville, TN.

Science Fiction

Setting:

Characters:

Attributes of Science Fiction

☐ The action takes place in the future or in another dimension.

☐ The premise of the story is scientifically imaginable.

☐ There is some travel through space.

☐ Robots or aliens are characters in the story.

Impossible Events:

IP 925-1 • *Graphic Organizers for Reading*
Copyright © 2006 by Incentive Publications, Inc., Nashville, TN.

Name _____

Biographies

Subject:

Attributes of Biographies

☐ Story of a real person

☐ Gives facts about where and when the person lived

☐ Explains what the person is remembered for

☐ Tells important events in the person's life

Description:

Interesting Facts:

Contributions:

A Question You Would Ask:

Name _____

IP 925-1 • *Graphic Organizers for Reading*
Copyright ©2006 by Incentive Publications, Inc., Nashville, TN.

Animal Stories

Setting:

Attributes of Animal Stories

☐ The main characters are animals.

☐ The animals are realistic.

☐ The animals are imaginary.

Characters:

Realistic Elements:

Fictional Elements:

Name _____

IP 925-1 • *Graphic Organizers for Reading*
Copyright ©2006 by Incentive Publications, Inc., Nashville, TN.

Fables

Characters:

Attributes of Fables

☐ The purpose of the story is to teach a lesson.

☐ There is a moral at the end.

☐ The story is short.

Action:

Lessons Taught:

Moral:

Name _____

IP 925-1 • Graphic Organizers for Reading

Fairy Tales

Setting:

Attributes of Fairy Tales

☐ Good Characters and evil characters

☐ Royalty and/or castle

☐ Special beginning and/or ending:
Once upon a time… and they lived happily ever after

☐ Magic

☐ Problem and solution

☐ Things happen in threes or sevens

Good Characters:

Bad Characters:

Magic:

Summary of Story:

Name _____

IP 925-1 • *Graphic Organizers for Reading*
Copyright © 2006 by Incentive Publications, Inc., Nashville, TN.

Fantasy

Setting:

Characters:

Attributes of Fantasy

- ☐ The setting of the story is not realistic.
- ☐ Story elements are make-believe.
- ☐ The events could not happen in reality.
- ☐ Animals or "things" talk.

Elements of Fantasy:

Name _____

IP 925-1 • *Graphic Organizers for Reading*
Copyright ©2006 by Incentive Publications, Inc., Nashville, TN.

Historical Fiction

Setting:

Characters:

Summary of Action

Historical Significance

Name _____

Humor

Characters:

Attributes of Humor

☐ The dialogue made me smile.

☐ The characters made me smile.

☐ The events made me smile.

Funny Events:

What Makes It Funny?

Name _____

IP 925-1 • *Graphic Organizers for Reading*

Blank
Graphic Organizers

Add Your Own Categories

Double Venn 54

Triple Venn 55

Wheel 56

Cluster 57

Two-Column 58

Three-Column 59

Four-Column 60

Bow Tie 61

Circle-Ray 62

Hand 63

Star 64

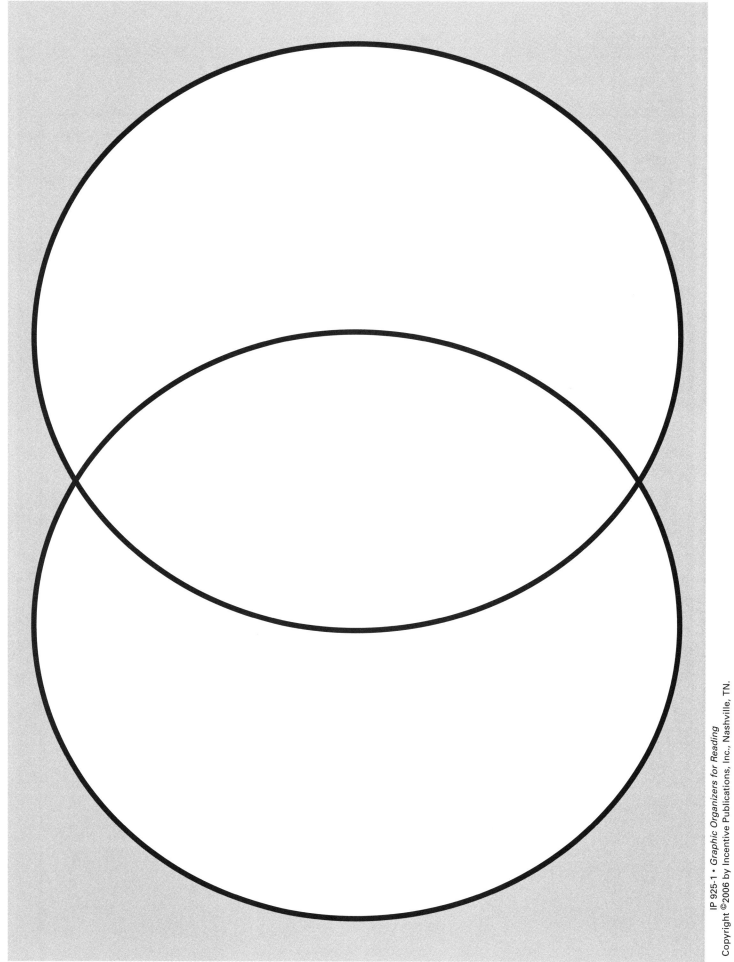

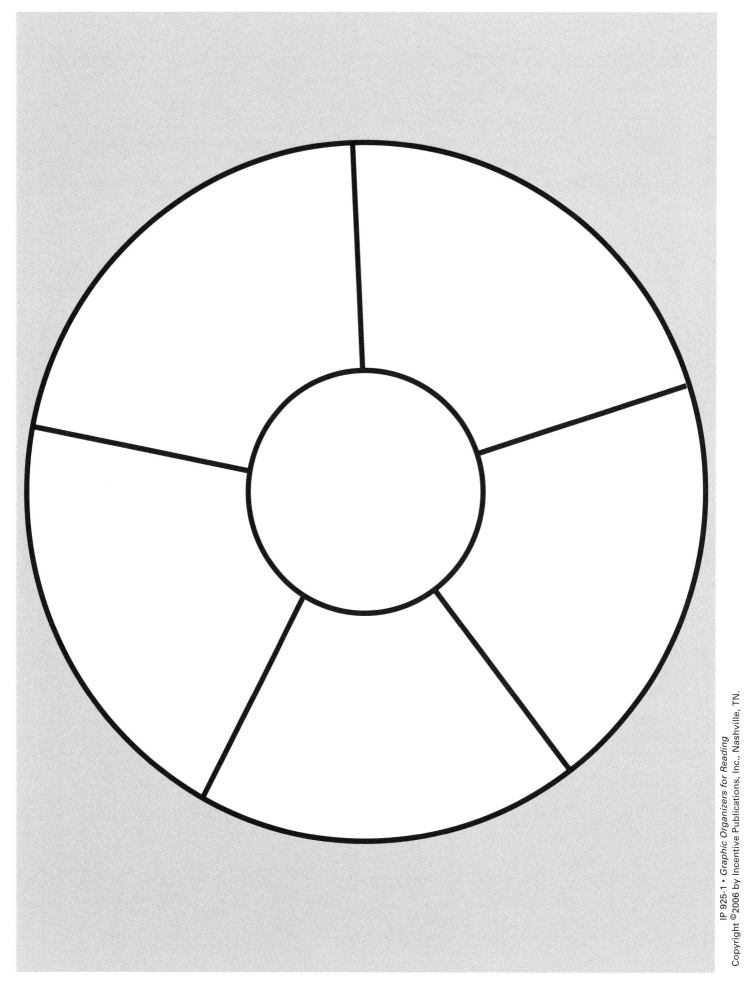

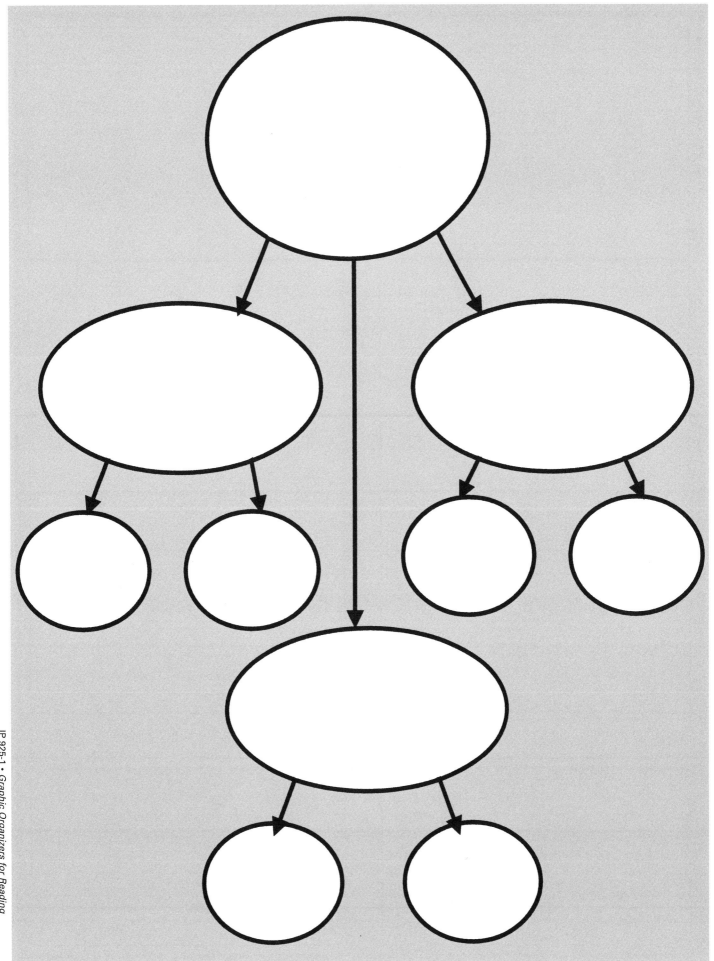

IP 925-1 • *Graphic Organizers for Reading*

IP 925-1 • *Graphic Organizers for Reading*

IP 925-1 • *Graphic Organizers for Reading*
Copyright © 2006 by Incentive Publications, Inc., Nashville, TN.

IP 925-1 • *Graphic Organizers for Reading*

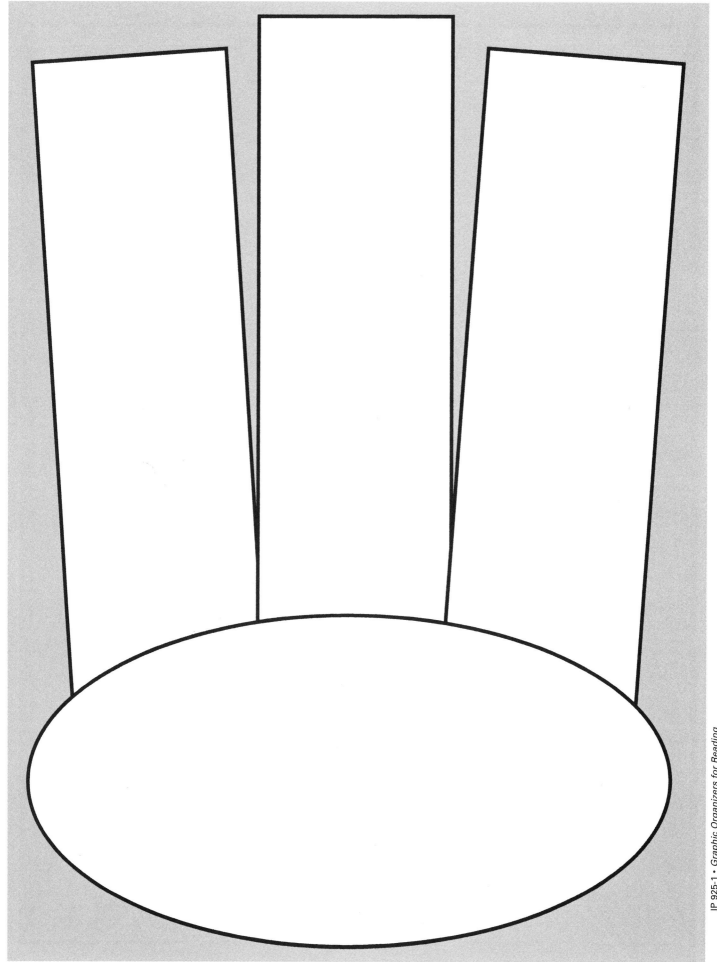

IP 925-1 • *Graphic Organizers for Reading*
Copyright ©2006 by Incentive Publications, Inc., Nashville, TN.

IP 925-1 • *Graphic Organizers for Reading*

64

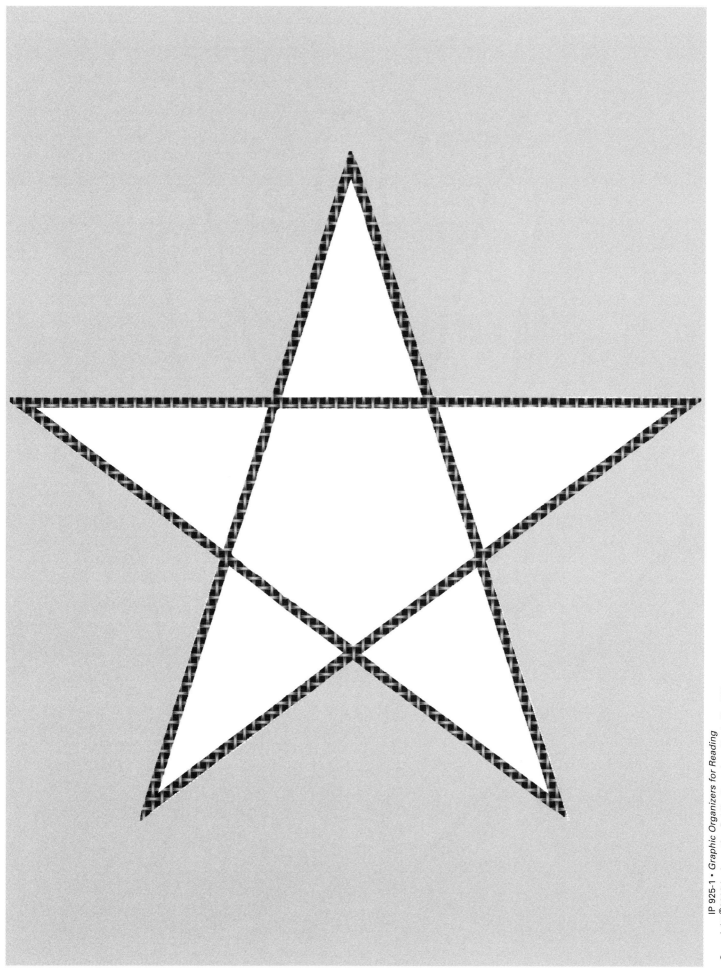